<u>Other FINKSTROM books in development:</u>

THE NEXT TO THE LAST OF THE MOHICANS
... just because we stole their land doesn't
mean we stole their sense of humor!

YOUR KAMPH OR MEIN?
... proving, once again, that three Reichs do
make a wrong!

SHEET FOR BRAINS
... the KKK and their on-going struggle to find
a good-fitting uniform!

FINKSTROM - "THE NEXT DEGENERATION"
... whether the subject is sports, psychology,
religion or proctology...no one is safe in the
world of Finkstrom!

For information, write: **Finkstrom Productions**
16526 West 78th Street
Suite 340
Eden Prairie, MN 55346
1-800-86-COMIC
(26642)

ATTENTION SCHOOLS AND BUSINESSES:
Finkstrom Productions offers quantity discounts with
bulk purchases for educational, business or sales
promotional use.

Library of Congress Catalog Card Number: 9561724

ISBN: 1-888016-00-0

Printed in the U.S.A.

This book
is dedicated to the millions
of business Frequent Flyers
who routinely suffer the multiple
indignities of flight in the hope
that humor, sarcasm, cynicism
and vindictiveness will help
lighten the load without having
to toss their luggage overboard.
If, in spite of our best efforts,
you find this book the least bit
offensive or in bad taste...you're
just not flying often enough.

"BEFORE YOU SIT DOWN, I THINK YOU SHOULD KNOW THAT I HAVE A NUMBER OF DISGUSTING HYGENIC HABITS."

"GREAT NEWS, CHIEF, BOTH AMELIA EARHART
AND JIMMY HOFFA HAVE BEEN FOUND...
IN A HOLDING PATTERN OVER O'HARE!"

ONLY THE FLYING WALENDAS HAVE
MASTERED THE ART OF GETTING TO THE
LAVATORY DURING MEAL SERVICE.

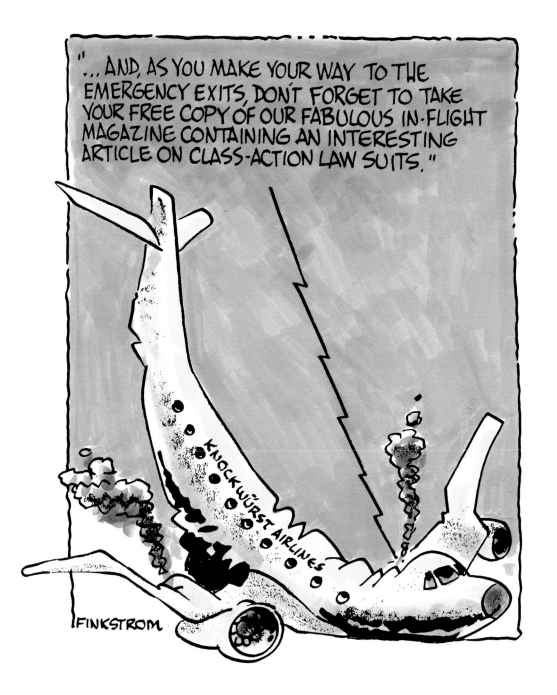

GOURMET GOURMOND

I ASKED FOR 1876, NOT 1886 FOR THE LAFEYETTE ROTHSCHILD WINE, AND THIS PATÉ IS FROM THE WRONG FRENCH PROVINCE.

WELCOME TO KNOCKWURST FLIGHT 626... DO YOU PREFER GREEN OR GRAY GRAVY ON YOUR MEAT-LIKE SUBSTANCE? CAN I BRING YOU A GLASS OF OLD SPICE ON THE ROCKS?

FINKSTROM

"YOU AND YOUR DISCOUNT TRAVEL AGENT DEALS."

"IN THE EVENT OF SUDDEN LOSS OF POWER, THE EMERGENCY LIGHTS WILL ILLUMINATE, ALLOWING YOU TO CRAWL ON YOUR HANDS AND KNEES TO THE NEAREST EXIT. IN THE EVENT OF A SUDDEN LOSS OF OXYGEN, THE MASK WILL FALL FROM THE CABINET ABOVE YOU, AND YOU CHOOSE TO PUT IT ON YOURSELF, OR USE IT FOR YOUR SPOUSE OR CHILDREN... NEXT, IN THE EVENT OF AN UNLIKELY WATER LANDING, YOUR SEAT IS A FLOATATION DEVICE AND ALSO CONTAINS SHARK REPELLENT... NOW THEN, JUST SETTLE BACK, RELAX AND ENJOY YOUR FLIGHT."
KNOCKWÜRST
FINKSTROM

HIGH PLANES DRIFTER.

"ARE YOU THE GUY WHO ORDERED THE
VEGETARIAN MEAL?"

" REMEMBER...SMOKING IN THE LAVATORIES OR TAMPERING WITH THE SMOKE DETECTION DEVICES ARE FEDERAL OFFENSES PUNISHABLE BY DEATH...OR TEN FREE FLIGHT PASSES ON OUR AIRLINES."

"EUNICE, NO NEED TO ANNOUNCE CONNECTING GATES AT ANY OF OUR 'HUBS'... EXCEPT FOR THOSE PASSENGERS WHO HAVE FINISHED THIRD OR BETTER IN THE HUNDRED METER OLYMPIC TRIALS."

"WE ALWAYS ALLOW FOUR HOURS
FLIGHT TIME ON NON-STOPS BETWEEN
CHICAGO AND MILWAUKEE...HOW ELSE
CAN WE GUARANTEE ANOTHER
'ON-TIME ARRIVAL'.?"

"FLOATATION DEVICE, MY ASS... IF THIS PLANE MAKES A WATER LANDING, MY SEAT CUSHION IS MORE LIKELY TO BE A TOILET!"

"LET'S ASSUME I'M HAVING DINNER WITH A COUPLE OF JAPANESE BUSINESSMEN... WHAT'S THE APPROPRIATE PROTOCOL IF ONE OF THEM FARTS?"

"HAVE YOU NOTICED THAT EVERYTIME WE'RE FORCED DOWN IN SHARK-INFESTED WATERS THE PASSENGERS GET SO 'CRANKY'?"

PLEASE RING YOUR CABIN ATTENDANT CALL BUTTON IF YOU WISH TO ENTER TONIGHT'S "NAME-THAT-SCIENCE-EXPERIMENT" DINNER SPECIAL.
FINKSTROM

"I MUST REMIND YOU, SIR...SMOKING ISN'T PERMITTED IN THE LAVATORY. HOWEVER, WE HAVE POSTED INSIDE THE DOOR A SUGGESTED LIST OF ALTERNATIVE ACTIVITIES."

FINKSTROM

"RELAX, THERE'S NOTHING TO BE AFRAID OF...
THERE IS NO MEAL SERVICE ON THIS FLIGHT."

"THE GENTLEMAN IN BUSINESS CLASS WOULD LIKE
TO KNOW OUR NEW E.T.A."